LANGUAGE ARTS EXPLORER JUNIOR

How to Write a How-To

by Cecilia Minden
and Kate Roth

CHERRY LAKE PUBLISHING • ANN ARBOR, MICHIGAN

Published in the United States of America by Cherry Lake Publishing
Ann Arbor, Michigan
www.cherrylakepublishing.com

Content Adviser: Jeannette Mancilla-Martinez, EdD, Assistant Professor of
Literacy, Language, and Culture, University of Illinois at Chicago

Design and Illustration: The Design Lab

Photo Credits: Page 5, ©Kamira/Shutterstock, Inc.; page 6, ©Susan
Leggett/Dreamstime.com; page 8, ©Martine De Graaf/Dreamstime.com;
page 11, ©Jonathan Ross/Dreamstime.com; page 14, ©Rob Marmion/
Shutterstock, Inc.; page 21, ©Dmitriy Shironosov/Shutterstock, Inc.

Library of Congress Cataloging-in-Publication Data
Minden, Cecilia.
  How to write a how-to/by Cecilia Minden and Kate Roth.
    p. cm.—(Language arts explorer junior)
  Includes bibliographical references and index.
  ISBN 978-1-61080-307-6 (lib. bdg.)—ISBN 978-1-61080-312-0
(e-book)—ISBN 978-1-61080-317-5 (pbk.)
1. English language—Composition and exercises—Juvenile literature.
I. Roth, Kate. II. Title. III. Series.
  PE1408M5623 2012
  808'.042—dc23   2011030943

Cherry Lake Publishing would like to acknowledge the work
of The Partnership for 21st Century Skills. Please visit
www.21stcenturyskills.org for more information.

Printed in the United States of America
Corporate Graphics Inc.
January 2012
CLSP10

Table of Contents

CHAPTER ONE

How Did They Do That?

Following instructions is a great way to learn new skills.

Think of all the things you know how to do. Can you tie your shoes? Do you know how to make your bed? You might know how to make a paper airplane. Do you think you could teach someone else how to do one of these things?

Writing how to do something takes careful planning. You need to include all of the **instructions**. A missing step will keep you from reaching your goal. Imagine baking a cake and leaving out the sugar. How would it taste? You are going to learn how to write instructions that are complete and easy to follow. Let's get started!

Plan your instructions step-by-step.

CHAPTER TWO

You Can Do That!

Coaches instruct their teams how to play sports.

We all know how to do many things. We sometimes forget that we had to learn how to do them. For example, you had to learn how to read the words on this page!

What can you do that other people might like to learn how to do? Think about your hobbies or a chore you do at home. Do you think you could teach someone how to do one of them? Think carefully! **Instructing** others is sometimes harder than it seems.

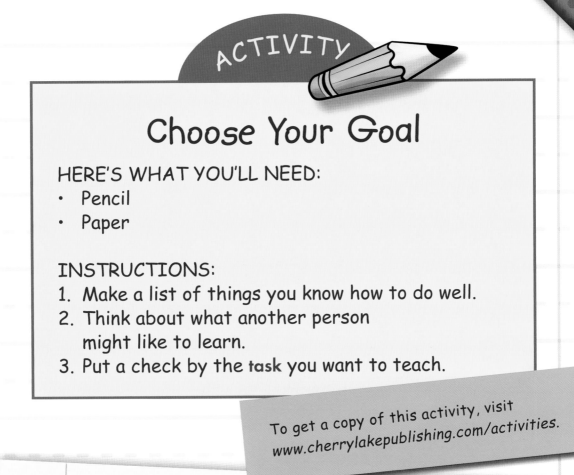

Choose Your Goal

HERE'S WHAT YOU'LL NEED:
- Pencil
- Paper

INSTRUCTIONS:
1. Make a list of things you know how to do well.
2. Think about what another person might like to learn.
3. Put a check by the **task** you want to teach.

To get a copy of this activity, visit www.cherrylakepublishing.com/activities.

WHAT CAN I DO?
- Fly a kite
- Ride a bike
- ✓ Make a jam sandwich
- Brush my teeth
- Play checkers

Reading other how-tos may help you learn how to write them.

CHAPTER THREE

What You Need

What materials will your project need?

Instructions usually begin with a list of materials. Set out all of the materials someone will need when following your instructions. It will be easier to write your list if you are looking at the items.

Write the name of each item on your list. You do not need to write complete sentences. Be **specific** when you describe your materials. Include the color, size, and amount of what the reader will need. That will make it easier for the reader to copy what you've done. Let's say you are teaching someone how to make a paper airplane. Write down the exact size of paper that will be needed.

The size of the paper used for this plane is perfect!

Gather Materials

HERE'S WHAT YOU'LL NEED:
- Pencil
- Paper
- Items needed for instructions

INSTRUCTIONS:
1. Gather the materials you need to teach someone how to do the task.
2. Write a list of the materials your reader will need. Write them in the order that they will be used.
3. If needed, include the color, size, and amount of each item.

Food materials are called ingredients. A set of instructions for cooking is called a recipe.

Mention every item someone would need for the project.

MATERIALS:
- plate
- butter knife

INGREDIENTS:
- jam
- butter
- bread

To get a copy of this activity, visit www.cherrylakepublishing.com/activities.

CHAPTER FOUR

Step-by-Step

Now it is time for the most important part of writing instructions. You must explain everything the reader needs to do to finish the task. Go step-by-step. Number each of the steps. This will help the reader understand the exact order in which to do them.

Think about the ways your teachers help you learn things at school.

Make sure you give clear instructions. Your readers will not be able to ask you questions. You need to explain clearly what to do. Let's say you are teaching someone to make a sandwich. You write, "Put the jam on the bread." A reader might put a jar of jam on top of a loaf of bread. That is not what you mean!

I don't think this is what you meant!

Write the Steps in Order

HERE'S WHAT YOU'LL NEED:
- Pencil
- Paper

INSTRUCTIONS:
1. Write out each step a reader needs to follow to complete the task.
2. Number each step so the instructions are in order.

To get a copy of this activity, visit www.cherrylakepublishing.com/activities.

How to Make a Jam Sandwich
1. Place two slices of bread side by side on a plate.
2. Take the lid off the jam jar.
3. Put jam on one side of one piece of bread.
4. Take the lid off the butter dish.
5. Put butter on one side of the second slice of bread.
6. Put one slice of bread on top of the other slice.
7. Use the knife to cut the bread in half.

CHAPTER FIVE

Use Details!

Reviewing your work is an important step in any writing project.

Now you have the steps written in order. It is time to go back to edit your words to make them more specific.

Use action words. Action words help readers understand exactly what you want them to do. For example, what actions do you use to make a sandwich? Do you *place* the bread on the plate? Do you *spread* the butter? Do you *scoop* up the jam?

You also need to include details about what the reader needs to do. For example, "Use the butter knife to spread 1 tablespoon of jam on one side of one slice of bread."

Add Details and Action Words

HERE'S WHAT YOU'LL NEED:
- Pencil
- Paper or Computer

INSTRUCTIONS:
1. Reread each line of your instructions.
2. Begin each line with an action word.
3. Add any details you think will help make your **directions** more clear.

To get a copy of this activity, visit www.cherrylakepublishing.com/activities.

HOW TO MAKE A JAM SANDWICH

Materials:
- A small clean plate
- A butter knife
- Two measuring spoons: a tablespoon and a teaspoon

Ingredients:
- 2 slices of bread
- 1 tablespoon of jam
- 2 teaspoons of soft butter

Directions:
1. Place two slices of bread side by side on a plate.
2. Remove the lid from the jam jar.
3. Use the tablespoon to scoop the jam from the jar.
4. Place the jam on one side of one piece of bread.
5. Use the knife to spread the jam so it covers the top of the bread.
6. Remove the lid from the butter dish.
7. Use the teaspoon to scoop two spoonfuls of butter onto the other slice of bread.
8. Use the knife to spread the butter over the top of the slice of bread.
9. Place one piece of bread on top of the other so the butter and jam are in the middle.
10. Use the knife to cut the bread in half.
11. Enjoy your jam sandwich!

CHAPTER SIX

See What I Mean?

Have you ever heard the saying "A picture is worth a thousand words"? Pictures can give readers a clear idea of what to do. A recipe often has photographs of exactly how to prepare the dish. Directions for how to put together a toy may have a picture of each step. The pictures help you see what the toy will look like as you build it.

You may want to draw pictures for your how-to. These are called illustrations. You can also ask someone to take photographs while you go through the steps. Include the pictures with your instructions.

Say "CHEESE!"

To get a copy of this activity, visit
www.cherrylakepublishing.com/activities.

ACTIVITY

Include Pictures

HERE'S WHAT YOU'LL NEED:
- Colored pencils
- Paper
- Camera (if using photographs)

INSTRUCTIONS:
1. Decide if you will use drawings or photographs with your directions.
2. Illustrate some of the steps of your instructions.

Make sure your drawings are clear and detailed.

HOW TO MAKE A JAM SANDWICH

Materials:
- A small clean plate
- A butter knife
- Two measuring spoons: a tablespoon and a teaspoon

Ingredients:
- 2 slices of bread
- 1 tablespoon of jam
- 2 teaspoons of soft butter

Directions:

1. Place two slices of bread side by side on a plate.
2. Remove the lid from the jam jar.
3. Use the tablespoon to scoop the jam from the jar.
4. Place the jam on one side of one piece of bread.
5. Use the knife to spread the jam so it covers the top of the bread.
6. Remove the lid from the butter dish.
7. Use the teaspoon to scoop two spoonfuls of butter onto the other slice of bread.
8. Use the knife to spread the butter over the top of the slice of bread.
9. Place one piece of bread on top of the other so the butter and jam are in the middle.
10. Use the knife to cut the bread in half.
11. Enjoy your jam sandwich!

CHAPTER SEVEN

Final Changes

You're almost finished. It is time to check everything one more time. Read your instructions carefully.

STOP! DON'T WRITE IN THE BOOK!

ACTIVITY

Checklist

☐ YES ☐ NO Did I list all of the materials?

☐ YES ☐ NO Did I put the steps in order?

☐ YES ☐ NO Did I number the steps?

☐ YES ☐ NO Did I include details and action words?

☐ YES ☐ NO Did I follow the instructions to make sure everything was included?

☐ YES ☐ NO Did I include pictures or illustrations?

☐ YES ☐ NO Did I check for correct spelling and grammar?

To get a copy of this activity, visit www.cherrylakepublishing.com/activities.

Now share your how-to with a friend!

Do It Yourself!

Go through the instructions as if you are the reader. Complete each action exactly as written. Did you include every step that is needed? Did you use enough detail to make your writing clear? You may want to ask a parent to try out your instructions first. Then you can share them with others.

What else can you teach others to do?

Glossary

directions (duh-REK-shuhnz) instructions for how to do something

how-tos (how-TOOZ) books, videos, or other things that teach how to do something

illustrations (il-uh-STRAY-shuhnz) pictures in a book, magazine, or other document

ingredients (in-GREE-dee-uhntz) items used to make something

instructing (in-STRUHKT-ing) teaching

instructions (in-STRUHK-shuhnz) directions on how something is done

photographs (FOH-tuh-grafs) pictures taken with a camera

recipe (RES-uh-pee) instructions for preparing food

specific (spuh-SIF-ik) clear, exact

task (TASK) a chore or piece of work to be done

For More Information

BOOKS

Benke, Karen. *Rip the Page! Adventures in Creative Writing*. Boston: Trumpeter, 2010.

Davis, Todd. *Handy Dad: 25 Awesome Projects for Dads and Kids*. San Francisco: Chronicle Books, 2010.

Twohy, Mike. *Poindexter Makes a Friend*. New York: Simon and Schuster, 2011.

WEB SITES

Fun English Games—Fun Writing Games for Kids
www.funenglishgames.com/writinggames.html
Explore interactive games to help you with your writing skills.

Professor Pen's Favorite Word Games
On-Line to Improve Writing Skills
www.writing-for-kids.com/wordgames.html
Find links to word games that will help you build your vocabulary.

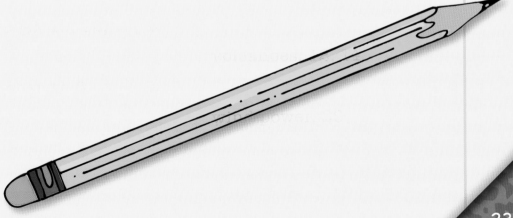

Index

About the Authors

Cecilia Minden, PhD, is the former director of the Language and Literacy Program at Harvard Graduate School of Education. She earned her doctorate from the University of Virginia. While at Harvard, Dr. Minden also taught several writing courses. Her research focuses on early literacy skills and developing phonics curriculums. She is now a full-time literacy consultant and the author of more than 100 books for children. Dr. Minden lives with her family in Chapel Hill, North Carolina. She likes to write early in the morning while the house is still quiet.

Kate Roth has a doctorate from Harvard University in language and literacy and a master's degree from Columbia University Teachers College in curriculum and teaching. Her work focuses on writing instruction in the primary grades. She has taught kindergarten, first grade, and Reading Recovery. She has also instructed hundreds of teachers from around the world in early literacy practices. She lives in Shanghai, China, with her husband and three children, ages 3, 7, and 10. Together they do a lot of writing to stay in touch with friends and family and to record their experiences.